# days

## TO
## CONTAGIOUS
## LIVING

# 31 days
## TO
## CONTAGIOUS
## LIVING

A DAILY DEVOTIONAL
GUIDE ON MODELING
CHRIST TO OTHERS

R. LARRY MOYER

**Kregel**
*Publications*

*31 Days to Contagious Living: A Daily Devotional Guide on Modeling Christ to Others*

© 2000 by R. Larry Moyer

Published by Kregel Publications, a division of Kregel, Inc., P.O. Box 2607, Grand Rapids, MI 49501.

Unless otherwise noted, Scripture quotations are from the New King James Bible Version. Copyright © 1979, 1980, 1982, Thomas Nelson, Inc., Publishers.

**Library of Congress Cataloging-in-Publication Data**
Moyer, R. Larry (Richard Larry).
31 days to contagious living: a daily devotional guide on modeling Christ to others / R. Larry Moyer.
     p.     cm.
  1. Witness bearing (Christianity)—Prayer-books and devotions—English. 2. Devotional calendars. I. Title: Thirty-one days to contagious living. II. Title.
BV4520.M66     2000          242'.2—dc21     00-035725
                                                            CIP

ISBN 978-0-8254-3570-6

*Printed in the United States of America*
1  2  3  4  5 / 13  12  11  10  09

*To my fellow brothers and sisters in the family of God worldwide who want to live in a way that attracts people to Jesus Christ. May God use this book to encourage you in holy living, and may God use you to introduce multitudes to the Savior.*

# Preface

No doubt you've heard it said, "All we have to do is live the Christian life around non-Christians. That in itself will bring them to the Savior."

I could not disagree more. Even if you lived a perfect and Christlike life, it would not explain to the non-Christian *how* to come to Christ. An individual can observe a dedicated Christian for fifty years and be impressed beyond description. But until somebody *explains* the gospel to that person, he or she has no idea how to come to the Savior.

Evangelism, biblically defined, means sharing the gospel with the *intent* of seeing the other person trust Christ. Until we present the gospel through spoken or written witness and invite people to trust Christ, we have not evangelized them. Whether or not they come to Christ is ultimately God's responsibility. But our job as evangelists includes both information and invitation.

At the same time, no one would deny the importance of living a life that attracts non-Christians to the Savior. Paul the apostle alluded to that very need. He says in Philippians 2:14–15, "Do all things without complaining and disputing, that you may become blameless and harmless, children of God without fault in the midst of a crooked and perverse generation, among whom you shine as lights in the world." Then he adds, "Holding fast the word of life. . . ."

His point is rather simple. We ought to live in such contrast to our "crooked and perverse generation" that we are to the world what the sun is to the universe—a light. Then, as we hold forth the Word of Life, our lives will give credibility to our message. It is worth noting that Friedrich Nietzsche, famous years ago for proclaiming that God is dead, also reportedly said, "Show me first that you are redeemed and I'll listen to you talk about your Redeemer."

That is the purpose of this devotional—to help you live a contagious life around non-Christians, a life so different that it causes non-Christians to say, "Hey, he's got something I don't. I wonder what it is." *Living* Christ at the same time you are *sharing* Him will give your words greater meaning and impact.

May God see fit to use this book to bring you closer to the Savior and improve your witness to others. And may God use your life *and* your lips to impact others with the truth about the Son, whom to know is life eternal.

# 31
## days
### TO
## CONTAGIOUS
## LIVING

*Day 1*

## Complaining about my suffering deprives God of the opportunity to prove His greatness.

**To Read**

*And lest I should be exalted above measure by the abundance of the revelations, a thorn in the flesh was given to me, a messenger of Satan to buffet me, lest I be exalted above measure. Concerning this thing I pleaded with the Lord three times that it might depart from me. And He said to me, "My grace is sufficient for you, for My strength is made perfect in weakness." Therefore most gladly I will rather boast in my infirmities, that the power of Christ may rest upon me. Therefore I take pleasure in infirmities, in reproaches, in needs, in persecutions, in distresses, for Christ's sake. For when I am weak, then I am strong.*

—2 Corinthians 12:7–10

**To Consider**

Suffering is painful. It causes us to adjust our schedules, reduce our workloads, and restrict our activities. We might be tempted to ask, "Why me?"

Paul speaks candidly about the thorn in his flesh. Many Bible teachers believe it was an eye ailment, because Paul refers to the large letters with which he wrote his epistles (Gal. 6:11). Vision problems would certainly have entailed suffering for someone of Paul's vigor and devotion. Three times he asked the Lord to remove it, and three times God said "No."

Instead, the Lord told him, "My grace is sufficient for you, for My strength is made perfect in weakness." Paul gained a whole new perspective on suffering. It became an opportunity for God to manifest His power. Suffering caused Paul to be grateful not only for the thorn in his flesh but also for trials of any kind. He testifies to the power of God: "Therefore I take pleasure in infirmities, in reproaches, in needs, in persecutions, in distresses for Christ's sake. For when I am weak, then I am strong."

Because non-Christians don't have that power available to them, it's understandable when they get upset, angry, and bitter. When they witness our acceptance and steadfastness, even in the face of disappointment, they can see the sustaining strength that belongs to God. Complaining about my suffering deprives God of the opportunity to prove His greatness.

### To Illustrate

In his book *The Problem of Pain,* C. S. Lewis writes, "God whispers to us in our pleasures, speaks in our conscience, but shouts in our pains: it is His megaphone to rouse a deaf world."

### To Meditate

There is never a hurt so strong that His grace is not stronger.

### To Pray

When you encounter suffering, ask God to help you so focus on His grace that you experience strength in the midst of weakness—a strength that causes non-Christians to ask, "How?" and "Why?"

*If God wanted me to carry a load of anxiety, He would have given me broader shoulders.*

**To Read**

> *Casting all your care upon Him, for He cares for you.*
>
> —1 Peter 5:7

**To Consider**

Anxiety has become the national pastime. We even offer excuses for our worrying, like the person who said, "Don't tell me worrying doesn't do any good. Everything I worry about doesn't happen."

Christians aren't exempt from the causes of worry—finances, illness, work, transportation, family issues, and education—but as believers, we do not have to let our legitimate *concerns* affect our nerves and become *anxiety*.

Two things are worth noting when Peter says, "Casting all your care upon Him, for He cares for you." One is that the word *care* is sometimes translated "worry." When so translated, it means to have a *distracting* care—the kind that keeps us awake at night and ties knots in our stomachs. Second, "cast" means that I can throw anything and everything that concerns me onto His shoulders. I can do my part—seek wise counsel and try to make responsible decisions—but without fretting the "what ifs," because those are on His shoulders.

What makes "casting our cares" so inviting? Peter sums it up in five words: "For He cares for you." Jesus, who died for me, also watches over me. In light of His almighty love and awesome power, it is senseless for me to worry.

The result of "casting our cares" is striking. Contrary to those around me, I can let life come my way, handling concerns as best I can while refusing to let them become anxieties. Anxieties are God's business. If God wanted me to carry a load of anxiety, He would have given me broader shoulders.

**To Illustrate**

A writer for *Our Daily Bread* told of a widow who successfully raised eighteen children—six biological children and twelve adopted ones. When asked how she managed to remain so calm and poised with her busy schedule, she said, "Oh, I'm in a partnership." "What kind of partnership?" she was asked. She answered, "One day, a long time ago, I said, 'Lord, I'll do the work, and You do the worrying.' I haven't had a worry since."

## To Meditate

People who live contagious lives are not exempt from concerns. They have simply learned how to handle their worry instead of letting worry handle them.

## To Pray

Ask God to help you handle your concerns with thoughtful action. But also ask Him to help you recognize when your concerns become distracting cares and to help you throw those cares on His shoulders.

## *Love means putting others first, even if it means sacrificing ourselves.*

**To Read**

> *In this the love of God was manifested toward us,*
> *that God has sent His only begotten Son into the*
> *world, that we might live through Him. In this is*
> *love, not that we loved God, but that He loved us*
> *and sent His Son to be the propitiation for our sins.*
> *Beloved, if God so loved us, we also ought to love*
> *one another.*
>
> —1 John 4:9–11

**To Consider**

A fireman rescues a would-be victim then suc-
cumbs to the blazing inferno. A swimmer, attempt-
ing to save a drowning child, becomes a victim of
the swift current. Few substitutionary deaths are in-
tentional. Most are accidental.

The death of Christ, however, was a *planned*
substitution. Sin must be punished, and the only

appropriate punishment is death. But one sinner cannot die for another, so God sent His perfect Son into the world to pay the penalty for sin on our behalf. Through Christ's death on the cross and His resurrection on the third day, God established a basis by which He could pardon, not punish. Jesus Christ satisfied the righteous anger of God against our sin by dying in our place. Once the wrath of God had been satisfied, God was free to extend eternal life as a gift to all who trust His Son as their only means of righteousness.

Now that's love, when somebody else suffers in our place. John exhorts, "Beloved, if God so loved us, we also ought to love one another."

A Christian who demonstrates sacrificial love stands out like a lighted billboard on a dark night. When others are surprised by our love, we can explain that we learned the definition from Jesus. Love means putting others first, even if it means sacrificing ourselves.

**To Illustrate**

The elderly lady stepped aboard the train, and it was apparent that her clothing offered little protection against the winter wind. Her hunched shoulders, downcast eyes, bony hands, and cracked skin revealed her plight. At the next stop, an energetic young man, neatly dressed and immaculate in appearance, strode onto the train. He noticed the woman and observed her misery. Three stops later, as the train slowed, he stepped past the old woman, exited the train, and disappeared. But in the woman's lap lay his warm and beautiful, brown, leather gloves.

**To Meditate**

When others compare your love to God's, do they see similarities or differences?

**To Pray**

Ask God to cause your love for others to grow until they are first in importance and you are second. Also, ask Him to use your sacrificial love to introduce others to His sacrifice.

*God never meant for the Christian life to be lived on an island.*

**To Read**

> *And if one member suffers, all the members suffer with it; or if one member is honored, all the members rejoice with it. Now you are the body of Christ, and members individually.*
>
> —1 Corinthians 12:26–27

**To Consider**

Ask people what their deepest misery is, and many will answer with one word—loneliness. Most suicide notes basically say, "I am extremely lonely."

Christians have a two-word answer for the problem of loneliness—one another. The Bible says that one reason we need each other is to shoulder one another's troubles and triumphs. Using the analogy of the human body, Paul says that "the members should have the same care for one another." He continues, "And if one member suffers, all the members suffer with it; or if one member is honored, all the members rejoice with it."

Christian companionship means that we don't go through trouble alone, and when we are honored, someone else is excited with us. Our burdens seem half the weight and our triumphs twice as exciting.

Non-Christians are attracted to that kind of togetherness. They recognize it as something they are missing. Loneliness has permeated their lives and, try as they might, nothing fills the gap. The book of Acts records the story of the believers in Jerusalem who cared so much for one another during times of persecution that they sold their possessions and distributed to those in need. It's no wonder that they were "praising God and having favor with all the people. And the Lord added to the church daily those who were being saved" (Acts 2:47). They understood that God never meant for the Christian life to be lived on an island.

**To Illustrate**

A man had a dream in which every person at a great banquet had both arms in plaster casts. Unable to feed themselves, they grew frustrated—until they decided on a solution. When each person extended an arm across the table to feed the next person, they all enjoyed the sumptuous feast. Each acting alone made matters worse. Togetherness solved everyone's problem.

**To Meditate**

In the body of Christ, we should never think, "I can handle it myself." Instead, we should say, "We can handle it together."

**To Pray**

Ask God to use your gifts and abilities to contribute to the growth, unity, and, ultimately, the impact of your local body of believers. Ask Him to show you ways *this week* that you can contribute to a spirit of togetherness.

*Day 5*

# *When faced with temptations, the answer is escape, not excuses.*

## To Read

> *No temptation has overtaken you except such as is common to man; but God is faithful, who will not allow you to be tempted beyond what you are able, but with the temptation will also make the way of escape, that you may be able to bear it.*
>
> —1 Corinthians 10:13

## To Consider

Believers have at least one thing in common with non-Christians—we are all tempted. When we give in to temptation, we use excuses like "I couldn't help it," "The situation was too enticing," or "Everybody else was doing it." But God has a different way out for His people. He wants us to take His escape route.

In 1 Corinthians 10, Paul mentions the children of Israel in the Old Testament who never seemed to get the message. They had tasted the miraculous.

They had seen God put breakfast on their plates every morning. Though outnumbered in battle, they had watched God defeat His enemies. Yet despite all that God had done on their behalf, Paul characterizes the people as lustful, idolaters, sexually immoral, murmurers, and tempters of Christ.

When temptation comes, what advice does God give? Take His escape route. If tempted to steal, put another person in charge of the finances. When confronted with sexual temptation, avoid the individual who tempts you. If tempted to anger, count to two hundred instead of ten. One thing is certain—God is faithful. You can count on Him to *always* provide a way of escape.

When we take God's way of escape, we demonstrate to non-Christians that we regard two things very seriously—sin and holiness. We also remove any basis for them to say, "Christians are no different than anybody else." In language as big as life, we tell them, "When faced with temptations, the answer is escape, not excuses."

**To Illustrate**

J. Vernon McGee told of a mother who saw her son in the kitchen after she had given him explicit orders not to eat before dinner. When she asked, "What are you doing?" he replied, "I'm in the kitchen trying to avoid temptation." She said, "What do you mean?" He explained, "I'm trying to stay out of the cookie jar." She responded, "The best way to stay out of the cookie jar is to stay out of the kitchen."

**To Meditate**

People who live contagiously are those who make right choices when confronted with the possibility of wrong actions.

**To Pray**

Ask God to help you recognize temptations for what they are—an attempt by Satan to hinder your walk *and* your witness to non-Christians. When tempted, determine to take the escape route instead of the temptation.

*Day 6*

*People tell their stories best when their tongues are their servants instead of their masters.*

**To Read**

*For every kind of beast and bird, of reptile and crea-ture of the sea, is tamed and has been tamed by mankind. But no man can tame the tongue. It is an unruly evil, full of deadly poison.*

—James 3:7–8

**To Consider**

"The most dangerous animal in the world," it has been said, "has its den behind your teeth." James would undoubtedly agree! When God made man, He gave him dominion over the four types of ani-mals. Every kind has been tamed by man—whether the shark, the snake, the lion, or the bird. Regard-less of how powerful or dangerous they might be, animals are at the mercy of man.

But the dominion that man gained over the animals, he lost over himself. The same tongue that God made for communication can be used to tear others to shreds. Every individual has experienced the power and the poison of the tongue.

Only through the indwelling of the Holy Spirit can the tongue be brought under control and used to its highest end—to proclaim the message of the saving grace of Christ. The impact of the gospel message is strengthened when a believer's tongue is controlled by God and only utters truth, focuses on building up instead of tearing down, and seeks to extend help instead of harm. People with disciplined tongues will capture the attention of others, because their speech will be markedly different. People tell their stories best when their tongues are their servants instead of their masters.

**To Illustrate**

A young lady once said to John Wesley, "I think I know what my talent is. I think it is to speak my mind." Wesley replied, "I do not think God would mind if you buried that talent." Some talents impact non-Christians better when they are used. Other talents are best buried—especially misuse of the tongue.

**To Meditate**

It is always better to bite your tongue instead of letting it bite somebody else.

**To Pray**

Ask God to help you control your tongue, so that when the most dangerous animal in the world exits its den, you instruct it instead of it instructing you.

*Happiness in marriage comes not from learning to live with your mate, but by making it easier for your mate to live with you.*

## To Read

> *Wives, submit to your own husbands, as is fitting in the Lord. Husbands, love your wives and do not be bitter toward them.*

> —Colossians 3:18–19

## To Consider

Someone once said, "Marriage is easy. It's living together afterward that's tough." Problems arise when a person tries to find a mate he or she can live with. The emphasis in Scripture is not so much on *finding* the right mate as *being* the right mate. With that in mind, both wives and husbands are instructed on how to live.

God exhorts wives, "Submit to your own husbands,

as is fitting in the Lord." In Ephesians 5:22, Paul says that the submission of a wife to her husband ought to reflect her submission to Christ. Recognizing her husband as the head of the home, she is to live in submission to his authority.

But God doesn't stop there. The authority of the husband is not that of a dictator over his subjects. It is that of a loving leader. Paul says, "Husbands, love your wives and do not be bitter toward them." Biblical love means "putting the other person first." Christian love also recognizes that people make mistakes and need forgiveness. Love doesn't count wrongs, it covers them.

Many homes in our society are in turmoil. So when non-Christians see a marriage lived according to biblical principles, they are often surprised. "Don't you two ever fight?" they might ask. Husbands and wives who submit to each other know how to disagree without being disagreeable. They also demonstrate that the focus is being the right mate instead of finding the right mate. Demonstrating that focus often gives Christians the occasion to tell others about the Savior, who helps them be better spouses. Happiness in marriage comes not from learning to live with your mate, but by making it easier for your mate to live with you.

**To Illustrate**

*Bits & Pieces* once told of a couple who were having marital difficulties and went to see a marriage counselor. The counselor asked, "Don't you two have anything in common?" The wife answered, "Yes, neither of us can stand the other." For a good marriage, don't concentrate on being able to "stand the other person" but live so that your spouse can "stand you."

## To Meditate

People who live contagious lives ask, "How am *I* doing" before asking, "How is my *mate* doing?"

## To Pray

Ask God to use your home and your relationship with your spouse as an example of what happens when God is the center of a marriage. With Christ in your home on earth, you can attract others to His home in heaven.

*Day 8*

*Decide now what you want written on your tombstone, then live your life backward from there.*

**To Read**

> *The days of our lives are seventy years; and if by reason of strength they are eighty years, yet their boast is only labor and sorrow; for it is soon cut off, and we fly away. . . . So teach us to number our days, that we may gain a heart of wisdom.*
>
> —Psalm 90:10, 12

**To Consider**

Life has a way of flying by.

The psalmist notes the shortness of our days when he talks about the frailty of man. He states, "For all our days have passed away in Your wrath; we finish our years like a sigh" (Ps. 90:9).

Recognizing a life span of seventy or eighty years, what conclusion does he draw? "Teach us to number our days, that we may gain a heart of wisdom."

One Bible teacher takes that sentence so seriously that he has counted the days until his eightieth birthday. He strikes off each day on a calendar to remind himself to live wisely.

Life is short and ought to be taken seriously. Decide now how you'd like to be remembered, then live your life accordingly. Do you want your tombstone to read, "He was the head of his corporation," or, "She was the best in her field"? Or would you rather it reflect an important contribution you've made to life?

The psalmist encourages us to live lives full of purpose, direction, and meaning. As Christians, we know the answers to the questions that non-Christians struggle with: Who am I? Why am I here? Where am I going? A focused, purposeful, and meaningful life will be the envy of non-Christians, and it will open up opportunities for you to point them to the giver of life. Decide now what you want written on your tombstone, then live your life backward from there.

**To Illustrate**

Swedish chemist Alfred Nobel awoke one morning and read his own obituary in the local newspaper. It read, "Alfred Nobel, the inventor of dynamite, who died yesterday, devised a way for more people to be killed in a war than ever before, and he died a very rich man." It was Alfred's *older brother* who had died; a newspaper reporter had bungled the epitaph. But that account had a tremendous impact on Nobel, who decided he wanted to be remembered for something different. As a result, he initiated the Nobel Prize to reward individuals who foster peace. He said, "Every man ought to have the chance to correct his epitaph in midstream and write a new one."

**To Meditate**

If, at the end of your life, you want to say "I did," instead of "I wish," alter your course *today*.

**To Pray**

Ask God to help you think through *how* and *where* your life should count. Decide now what your tombstone ought to say and determine to live your life accordingly.

*Day 9* | *Trials, rightly faced, make us better, not bitter.*

**To Read**

*My brethren, count it all joy when you fall into various trials, knowing that the testing of your faith produces patience. But let patience have its perfect work, that you may be perfect and complete, lacking nothing.*

—James 1:2–4

**To Consider**

Non-Christians are immensely impressed when they see believers standing right side up while their world has turned upside down. Whether the trial results from a severe health problem, a car accident, financial difficulties, or a layoff at work, when we keep our chins up despite circumstances others say, "Whatever you've got, I need it."

James addresses people going through trials. These early believers had lost their possessions and had been separated from their loved ones as they were scattered throughout Asia Minor during a time of persecution.

They were tempted to become bitter and rebel against God. James speaks directly to the point: "Count it all joy when you fall into various trials."

Why joy? The reason is simple: "Knowing that the testing of your faith produces patience." Patience is an essential characteristic of Christlikeness. Without patience, our spiritual growth will never be mature and complete. And the only way patience can be produced is through trials. So James encourages us when he writes, "Let patience have its perfect work, that you may be perfect and complete, lacking nothing." Trials rightly faced make us better, not bitter.

**To Illustrate**

A man who now has a very effective full-time Christian ministry came to know Christ because a Christian girl he loved was killed in an automobile accident. The girl had shared Christ with him the very first time they met. When she died, what impressed him most was that her Christian parents were more concerned about how he would handle the tragedy than they were about themselves. He saw that they had something he didn't.

**To Meditate**

People whose lives become contagious are not those who always have the right things happen to them, but those who have the right response when the wrong things happen.

**To Pray**

Take a moment and thank God for the hard times you have experienced. If you've allowed bitterness to come into your life—toward God or toward others—confess it to Him as sin and ask Him to forgive you.

## Day 10

*Man's way of dealing with sin is denial or defense; God's way is declaration.*

### To Read

*For I acknowledge my transgressions, and my sin is always before me. Against You, You only, have I sinned, and done this evil in Your sight—that You may be found just when You speak, and blameless when You judge. . . . Create in me a clean heart, O God, and renew a steadfast spirit within me. . . . Restore to me the joy of Your salvation, and uphold me by Your generous Spirit. Then I will teach transgressors Your ways, and sinners shall be converted to You.*

—Psalm 51:3–4, 10, 12–13

### To Consider

Sin is extremely subtle—especially when it keeps sinners from facing their wrongdoing. Our usual way out is either denial or defense. We blame somebody else or rationalize that our responsibility is minor compared to that of the other person.

God's way for dealing with wrongdoing is declaration. Let's call it what He calls it: sin. The prophet Nathan made God's standard quite clear to King David in 2 Samuel 12, when he told David a parable to show him his sin. After David had condemned the obvious sinner in the parable, Nathan made the application by saying, "You are the man." David got the point and later wrote Psalm 51 as a testimony. He was forced to acknowledge to God, "Against You, You only, have I sinned, and done this evil in Your sight."

What makes such a declaration meaningful? When we deal with our sin God's way, we gain a clear conscience as a result. Upon his confession, David pleads, "Create in me a clean heart, O God" (v. 10). David also prays, "Restore to me the joy of Your salvation" (v. 12). Such joy makes us want even more to see non-Christians come to Christ. David continues, "Then I will teach transgressors Your ways, and sinners shall be converted to You" (v. 13).

Declaring sin to be what it is communicates two things to those around us—the seriousness of sin and the beauty of salvation. When we acknowledge our faults and waywardness, we communicate that we are genuine people. But we are also appreciative people who reflect our gratitude through the joy of His pardon and want others to experience that pardon.

Man's way of dealing with sin is denial or defense; God's way is declaration.

### To Illustrate

A boy handed his father his poor report card and asked, "Dad, what do you think my problem is—heredity or environment?" Does such a defensive comment remind you of anyone you know?

### To Meditate

If sin were not so serious, the cross of Christ would never have been necessary.

### To Pray

Acknowledge to God an area of wrongdoing that you are quick to deny or defend. Then call it what He calls it—sin—and ask Him to forgive you.

## Day 11

*Forgiveness has no limits, and neither should the privilege of extending it to somebody else be limited.*

### To Read

*Then Peter came to Him and said, "Lord, how often shall my brother sin against me, and I forgive him? Up to seven times?" Jesus said to him, "I do not say to you, up to seven times, but up to seventy times seven."*

—Matthew 18:21–22

### To Consider

We come to God as slanderers, adulterers, thieves, evil thinkers, and self-centered people. But as soon as we recognize our sinful condition and place our trust in Jesus Christ alone to save us, He loudly and clearly proclaims us forgiven. We are then released to live each day in the freedom of forgiveness instead of the torture of guilt.

Forgiveness does carry a measure of indebtedness

along with it, however—the privilege of extending that same forgiveness to somebody else. Peter no doubt thought he was being most generous by suggesting "seven times." The traditional rabbinic teaching held that an offended person need only forgive a brother three times. By His admonition of "seventy times seven," Jesus' point was unmistakable. Our offering of forgiveness to others ought not to have limits.

What greater way to show other people what God is like? Non-Christians—and even Christians at times—can be impatient, use abusive language, and take rather than give. When a person is offended, he or she often responds with revenge. How shocking it is, then, when a believer instead practices forgiveness. Forgiveness is the love of God translated into the language of daily life.

A forgiving attitude may annoy some non-Christians, because it destroys their basis for saying "Christians are just like everybody else." Nevertheless, forgiveness has no limits, and neither should the privilege of extending it to somebody else.

### To Illustrate

On July 1, 1992, a thirty-three-year-old attorney sat in a Fort Worth, Texas, courtroom preparing to present his case. Suddenly and without warning, a gunman burst into the courtroom and opened fire. A court official was killed instantly, and the attorney fled to get help. The gunman followed, caught the attorney in the stairway, and shot him dead.

After the killer's conviction, and just before his execution for the murders, the attorney's young widow, not wanting the gunman to suffer eternally for his sin, wrote him a letter explaining the gospel. She offered him her forgiveness and said she wanted him to experience the forgiveness of Christ. As he was led to his execution, he went as an individual who had trusted Christ.

**To Meditate**

Christians who live contagiously are those who, as forgiven people, recognize the privilege of forgiving others.

**To Pray**

Ask God to help you reflect on His forgiveness of you. Then ask Him to give you an opportunity *this week* to explain to a lost acquaintance the great forgiveness found in Christ.

*Day 12*

*People who are honest in this life can be trusted to be honest about life in the hereafter.*

**To Read**

*Open your hearts to us. We have wronged no one, we have corrupted no one, we have defrauded no one.*

—2 Corinthians 7:2

**To Consider**

Honesty and integrity are often cast as old-fashioned traits. It's easier to find a person who's as "phony as a three-dollar bill" than it is to find a person who is "solid as a rock." Far too often, even some Christians gain a reputation for dishonesty.

The apostle Paul's enemies attacked him relentlessly. At times they insinuated that he had harmed his converts and defrauded them, both spiritually and financially. Of course, quite the opposite was true. It was the false teachers who had injured the Corinthians with their corrupt doctrines and who perhaps had lived in Corinth at the people's expense.

Paul's integrity was his best rebuttal. He asked the

Corinthians to "open your hearts to us," or, in other words, "make room for us in your affections." His reason was straightforward. He had corrupted nobody, either morally or physically. In every matter, he was straight in his dealings. There had never been a single instance when the apostle's teaching or conduct had been dishonest or had a detrimental effect. People like Paul are easy to love, easy to appreciate.

A non-Christian neighbor once told me regarding his financial dealings, "I have two books—one underneath the table and one above the table." Believers who conduct their lives with honesty and integrity give non-Christians a basis not only to hear the truth but also to listen. The truth about the Savior is best communicated through the truthful lips of a disciple! People who are honest in this life can be trusted to be honest about life in the hereafter.

**To Illustrate**

In 1990, a London newspaper told of a man who found four million British pounds in negotiable bonds that had fallen from a messenger's briefcase into the gutter. With a salary of £12,000 a year and £2,500 in overdrafts, he was tempted to say "Finders keepers, losers weepers." He could have moved out of his one-bedroom apartment into the home of his dreams. "He could have gotten on a plane and gone anywhere," his girlfriend observed. "The world was his oyster." Instead, he returned the documents with a simple explanation. "I was brought up to be honest, so I had to give up my dream." Imagine the impact a Christian with that kind of integrity could have upon the lost.

## To Meditate

People who want the lost to trust the Savior ought to live in such a way that the lost can trust them.

## To Pray

Ask God to keep you so honest in your dealings with others that the message you have for the lost is enhanced by the integrity of your words and your life.

*Being out of control is a cinch, but those who impact others practice self-control.*

## To Read

> *Therefore, as the elect of God, holy and beloved, put on tender mercies, kindness, humbleness of mind, meekness, longsuffering.*
>
> —Colossians 3:12

## To Consider

According to Colossians 3:12, a child of God should be adorned with the garment of meekness. Meekness means to be considerate of others. The word was originally used of a wild horse that was brought under control with the use of bit and bridle. Therefore, meekness literally means "strength under control."

Meekness first and foremost applies to the way you respond when God allows hard moments to come into your life. Instead of becoming angry or bitter, do you submit to what He's trying to teach you?

Furthermore, meekness applies to how you respond to insults and injuries from others. A meek person recognizes that these, too, are allowed by God for a good purpose. Therefore, instead of lashing out or becoming revengeful, believers practice strength under control.

Three words often characterize non-Christians—out of control. They roll down the window and scream "Watch it, buddy!" when another driver intrudes into their traffic lane. They slam down the receiver when the party they are calling does not meet their demands. They blame everyone from the cashier to the store manager for the long lines in the grocery store. And when they arrive home from a hard day at work, their families become the victims of problems at the office.

To watch a believer practice self-control is rather stunning. "Where does he get such strength?" "How can he stay so calm?" A believer's credibility soars because of a simple fact: Being out of control is a cinch, but those who impact others practice self-control.

**To Illustrate**

Bible teacher Howard Hendricks once told of flying from Boston to Dallas on a plane that departed six hours late. It was a Friday afternoon, and several businessmen, weary from a long week and anxious to get home, were quite upset about the delay. One man angrily growled at the flight attendant every time she walked by. After observing this display, Hendricks walked back to the galley to commend the flight attendant for her self-control and the way she had handled a difficult situation. He asked for her name so that he could write the airline management to express his appreciation. "Oh," she exclaimed. "I don't work for American Airlines. I work for Jesus Christ."

## To Meditate

People who handle life well have learned through Christ how to handle themselves.

## To Pray

This week, whatever goes wrong—whether minor or major—ask God to enhance your witness by helping you get a grip on your own emotions.

## Day 14

*Believers who are properly focused turn their eyes outward, not inward.*

**To Read**

> *Let each of you look out not only for his own interests, but also for the interests of others.*
>
> —Philippians 2:4

**To Consider**

Selfishness permeates our society. "What's in it for me?" has become *the* philosophy to live by. Advertisers promote their products by asking, "Don't you deserve more?" or suggesting "You deserve the best."

Nowhere does the Bible discourage believers from considering their own interests. But the Bible does discourage believers from thinking *only* of themselves. Instead, as we consider our own needs, we ought also to consider the needs of others. Paul the apostle states it plainly, "Let each of you look out not only for his own interests, but also for the interests of others."

Such an idea was foreign to the Greek mind-set. Instead, people put themselves on pedestals, becoming self-seeking and self-promoting. But Christians ought to have Christ on the pedestal and in genuine Christlikeness focus on others, not merely on themselves. When considering activities with others, we should ask, "What would they enjoy?" rather than simply, "What would *I* enjoy?" When blessed with an extra loaf of bread, we might think of a neighbor before the freezer. Before running an errand, we could ask a neighbor, "Is there something I can pick up for you?"

People who are truly considerate are becoming increasingly rare. Unbelievers live and work around those whose only focus is themselves. When non-Christians meet such people, they may be surprised enough to ask "What makes them so different?" Believers who are properly focused turn their eyes outward, not inward.

### To Illustrate

Once there was a dog with a bone in his mouth. He crossed a stream on a small footbridge and, when he looked into the water, saw his reflection. Thinking it was another dog with a bone, he barked, trying to scare the other dog into dropping its bone. His own bone then fell into the water. Selfishness caused him to lose what he had. Selfishness hurts everyone, and for Christians, it can diminish their impact on non-Christians.

**To Meditate**

On a scale of one to ten, where would others place you when asked, "How others-centered is that person?"

**To Pray**

Ask God through His Holy Spirit to convict you of any areas of your life where your focus is solely on yourself. Then take practical steps this week to allow a change of thinking to create a change in focus.

*Day 15*

> *Anger is sometimes justifiable, as long as we control our anger instead of letting it control us.*

## To Read

> *"Be angry, and do not sin": do not let the sun go down on your wrath.*
>
> —Ephesians 4:26

## To Consider

Aristotle was noted for his comment, "Anyone can become angry. That is easy. But to be angry with the right person, to the right degree, at the right time, for the right purpose, and in the right way—that is not easy."

Aristotle was biblically correct. The Scriptures do not admonish us never to become angry. In certain situations, anger is both understandable and justifiable. The irresponsibility of an employee, lies told by a trusted friend, the disobedience of a child, the unfaithfulness of a mate, or a misrepresentation by a relative can cause us tremendous exasperation. If not controlled, such anger can lead to ill will, which can result in a grudge, which may lead to retaliation. In other words, uncontrolled anger can lead to everything except the kind of behavior that should represent Christian discipleship.

The answer Scripture gives is to keep short accounts. Our anger ought to cease on the same day it occurs. It shouldn't set any later than the sun.

Sometimes anger is so explosive that it makes the front-page news. A newspaper recently told of a father who confessed to the brutal beating and death of his three-year-old son. The father said, "He would not come when I told him to."

Christians who know how to manage their anger attract attention. Practicing self-control may give us opportunities to talk to non-Christians about the One who gives us control—the same One who became so angry at sin that He solved our problem by paying for our sins with His own blood. Anger is sometimes justifiable, as long as we control our anger instead of letting it control us.

**To Illustrate**

Alexander the Great deserved his name. He was noted for his energy and intelligence. There were times, however, when he victimized others with his anger. On one of those occasions, Cletus, his dear friend and general, became intoxicated and ridiculed the emperor in front of his men. Angrier than ever, Alexander snatched a spear from a soldier and threw it at Cletus, unintentionally killing him. Alexander was so overcome by grief that, had his men not stopped him, he would have taken his own life with the same spear. Though he conquered many cities, he never conquered his anger. In contrast, Christians become contagious when we demonstrate to others how to conquer anger instead of letting it conquer us.

## To Meditate

Your anger ought always to set the same day it arises.

## To Pray

Ask God to help you be certain that when you get mad it's about the right things. Furthermore, ask Him to help you be distinguished as a person whose anger has a short life.

## Day 16

*When we go through hard times, God does not promise answers, but He does promise His presence.*

**To Read**

*Yea, though I walk through the valley of the shadow of death, I will fear no evil; for You are with me; Your rod and Your staff, they comfort me.*

—Psalm 23:4

**To Consider**

The Christian life is not a bed of roses—and it was never designed to be. The same things that happen to others happen to us: crippling illnesses, layoffs at work, family struggles, car accidents, unexpected bills, and on and on.

During those times, we often wonder, "Why does God let this happen? Why should I be 'punished' as though I'm doing something wrong, when I'm trying to do what is right?" The Bible never answers these questions, even in the book of Job, in which a man who lived close to God's heart encountered tremendous hardships. The Bible simply tells us how to respond to hardships—positively, properly, and biblically.

The Scriptures also give words of comfort. In Psalm 23:4, David declares, "Yea, though I walk through the valley of the shadow of death, I will fear no evil; for You are with me; Your rod and Your staff, they comfort me." David had in mind the worst darkness that a flock of sheep would encounter—a deep ravine between two mountains or a narrow pass among the rocks. This is where wolves would lurk and snakes would hide to attack the sheep as they came along. To protect the flock, a shepherd always carried two implements—a rod and a staff. The rod was about two feet long and had a round knot on the end. He could use this to club any animal that endangered his sheep. The staff was much longer and had a rounded hook on the end. He could use this to swing branches out of the way or to pull a sheep out of a hole. From the sheep's perspective, the best protection was the presence of the shepherd.

As David reflects upon his own relationship to God as that of a sheep to the Good Shepherd, he recognizes a similar truth. When we experience trouble, it's the presence of the Shepherd that makes the difference.

Those around us need to see that when we go through hard times, we don't have all the answers.

But we have Jesus Christ—the One to whom we are personally related. He is there, uplifting, encouraging, strengthening, guiding, and loving us through anything we face. He will not abandon us. In fact, in times of trouble, He will be the closest He's ever been. James 4:8 encourages us: "Draw near to God and He will draw near to you."

God's presence makes the difference between those who stand up and those who fold up when hard times hit. We are able to go on—not because we don't feel the pain, but because we feel the comfort of His presence. When we go through hard times, God does not promise answers, but He does promise His presence.

**To Illustrate**

Joseph Scrivener was a young man in Ireland when, in 1840, his bride-to-be drowned the evening before their wedding. He began training as a military cadet, but poor health made him abandon such a career. He moved to Canada, where his second fiancée died following a brief illness. His life was filled with loneliness, meager pay, and physical illness. Yet it is he who wrote "What a friend we have in Jesus. . . . In His arms He'll take and shield thee, thou will find a solace there."

**To Meditate**

When contagious Christians experience hardship,

others can see how near they are to God—and how very near He is to them.

**To Pray**

Ask God to help you use the hard moments in your life as stepping-stones to know Him better and to experience His presence in a greater way than ever before.

*Love that says "I love you if . . ." is very common. Love that says "I love you, period" is very uncommon.*

**To Read**

*But I say to you who hear: Love your enemies, do good to those who hate you. . . . But if you love those who love you, what credit is that to you? For even sinners love those who love them.*

—Luke 6:27, 32

**To Consider**

There's nothing unusual about human love. We love people who love us, assist those who assist us, and favor those who may be useful to us in the future. It's the kind of love that can be found in just about anybody, anywhere. It is therefore no wonder that Jesus should say, "But if you love those who love you, what credit is that to you? For even sinners love those who love them."

Divine love is different and distinctively sets

people apart. Jesus exhorts us to rise above mere human love when He says "Love your enemies, do good to those who hate you." With His help, we can love those who don't love us back and do favors for people without expecting something in return. Instead of simply not rendering evil for evil, we can go a step further. We can do good to those who do wrong to us.

When non-Christians encounter this kind of unconditional love from Christians, they get a picture of what God is like, because love is the essence of God. Unconditional, sacrificial love grabs the attention of non-Christians. Love that says "I love you *if . . ."* is very common. Love that says "I love you, *period"* is very uncommon.

**To Illustrate**

*Time* magazine told of a woman whose son went to prison for fourteen years for a horrific sexual assault. Freed in 1994, he committed a string of crimes even more ghastly, which caused him to receive the title "the devil incarnate" and a sentence of fifty to one hundred years. In the article, his mother testified that the Bible got her through the day. Once a week for eighteen years, she has driven six hours, one way, to visit her son, and has only missed three times. The entire ordeal, including the time she spends inside the prison, is eighteen hours round-trip. The son, who admits he deserves to be in prison, says this about his mother: "Her love transcends whatever obstacle I've thrown in front of her." Our love, with God's grace, ought to transcend all obstacles thrown in front of us as well.

**To Meditate**

The love that reflects the love of Christ is always followed by a period, not by a condition.

**To Pray**

Think about the people with whom you have the most difficulty demonstrating love. As you reflect on Christ's love—which extended even to the people who crucified Him—ask God to make your love a copy of His and to use it specifically to impact non-Christians.

*Nonbelievers have a reason to listen to Christians whose lives mirror their preaching.*

## To Read

> *Brethren, join in following my example, and note those who so walk, as you have us for a pattern.*
> —Philippians 3:17

## To Consider

Non-believers often say, "Christians are hypocrites. They preach one thing, then practice another."

Sometimes that complaint is simply an excuse behind which the nonbeliever is trying to hide. Far too often, however, nonbelievers do see Christians whose lips say one thing and whose lives say another.

Paul the apostle was widely regarded as a single-minded person. His daily focus was to become more Christlike and to attain maturity in Christ. Therefore, as he sincerely endeavored to follow Christ, he could exhort others. When he said, "Brethren, join in following my example," Paul was not being conceited or self-righteous. Nor was he claiming that, spiritually, he was where he needed to be.

Instead, he was simply expressing what everybody could see. He was so consistent in his effort to become like Christ, he could say, "Follow me, because I'm following Christ." Paul recognized that there were other believers who could issue the same invitation: "And note those who so walk, as you have us for a pattern." Timothy and Epaphroditus were undoubtedly two others who practiced conduct not dictated by human regulations but by a personal relationship with Jesus Christ.

Imagine a non-Christian living or working next to Paul the apostle. What could anyone have pointed to that was not consistent with Christian character or conduct? Imagine, too, the opportunities and boldness that Paul had because his life supported his lips. Nonbelievers have a reason to listen to Christians whose lives mirror their preaching.

**To Illustrate**

A man about to be ordained was being questioned about his background and Christian experience. With a great deal of honesty and transparency, he explained how at one period of his life he was nearly an infidel. He then explained, "There was one argument in favor of Christianity that I could never refute—the consistent conduct of my own father!"

Could a non-Christian family member, neighbor, or coworker say of you, "There is one argument in favor of Christianity that I can never refute—the consistent conduct of that believer"?

## To Meditate

When it comes to drawing non-Christians to Christ, is your life an attraction or a distraction?

## To Pray

Ask God to show you any area of your life that is inconsistent with your Christian testimony. Acknowledge it as sin, ask Him to forgive you, and then take immediate steps to correct what is wrong.

*Day 19*

*Fathers who have a
positive impact on their
children specialize in
inspiration, not irritation.*

**To Read**

> *Fathers, do not provoke your children, lest they be-
> come discouraged.*

—Colossians 3:21

**To Consider**

Rearing children has been compared to holding a
wet bar of soap. If you squeeze too tightly, the soap
will shoot from your hand. If your hold on too
loosely, it slides away. A gentle yet firm grasp keeps
it in your control.

The Scriptures clearly teach that parents are to be
in authority in the home. Paul addresses fathers because, as the heads of their homes, they are ultimately
responsible before God for what happens within the
family. Paul's admonition helps fathers know what is
important in keeping the right hold on their children.

The apostle explains that fathers should not deal with their children in such a way as to irritate or arouse anger. Unrelenting unkindness, needless severity, continual agitation, unreasonable demands, and constant fault-finding cause children to become discouraged. Discouraged children lose heart and soon give up trying to please or do their best. They may go about their tasks in a listless, moody, sullen frame of mind. Children often need to be corrected, but they should be admonished in ways that help them understand the ultimate goal: to help and encourage them. Children should think of their parents as being on their team, not on their backs.

When you consider that every child is born a nonbeliever, you can see the potential impact of a parent's adherence to biblical principles. By raising their children in obedience to Christ, Christian parents can draw them to the Lord. Also, a child's impression of the heavenly Father is often determined by his impression of his human father. A father who properly loves and cares for his children portrays to the world an image of the heavenly Father. Fathers who have a positive impact on their children specialize in inspiration, not irritation.

**To Illustrate**

Once when the great composer and pianist Ignacy Jan Paderewski was performing at a great concert hall in America, a mother took her son to the concert.

Prior to Paderewski's performance, while the mother was distracted, the boy slipped away, attracted to the grand piano on the performance stage. Placing his trembling fingers on the keys, he began to play "Chopsticks." The crowd, irritated and embarrassed, shouted, "Get that boy away from there! Who would bring a kid that young here?" Hearing the commotion, Paderewski rushed onto the stage, reached around the boy and began to harmonize. As he did so, he murmured in the boy's ear, "Keep going . . . don't quit, son . . . keep on playing . . . don't stop."

**To Meditate**

Some parents simply provoke their children. Others provoke them to love and good works.

**To Pray**

Ask God to help you raise your children in such a way that, whether directing or disciplining, you are a source of encouragement, not discouragement.

*Day 20*

## We lose our fear of death when we see it as an exclamation point instead of a period.

### To Read

*"O Death, where is your sting? O Hades, where is your victory?" The sting of death is sin, and the strength of sin is the law. But thanks be to God, who gives us the victory through our Lord Jesus Christ.*

—1 Corinthians 15:55–57

### To Consider

Ted Turner once confessed in *Time* magazine that his life has been a struggle to master his greatest fear—the fear of death. He commented, "If you can get yourself where you're not afraid of dying, then you can . . . move forward a lot faster."

The fear of death is understandable. After all, one out of every one person dies! What gives death its sting is sin. Death came as a result of man's rebellion and disobedience against God. The law of God, as epitomized in the Ten Commandments, shows sin to be what it is—a fist in the face of God. Through the law, we know we are sinners who deserve eternal condemnation.

On the cross, God met victory, and Satan met defeat. Jesus Christ, the perfect Son of God, took the sinner's place and suffered the punishment that you and I deserved. On the third day, He arose as proof that He had conquered both sin and the grave. Through personal trust in Christ, we receive His free gift of eternal life. Consequently, we can live as people who are prepared to die, and die as people who are prepared to live.

Upon trusting Christ, we can exclaim with Paul the apostle, "O Death, where is your sting? O Hades, where is your victory?"

Non-Christians are often uncomfortable talking about death. As they drive past an accident, read the statistics on heart attacks or fatal diseases, or hear about the sudden death of a friend, the question haunts them, "What if it happened to me?" To see a Christian approach death without fear is often surprising to them. Many have come to Christ after they witnessed Christians at a funeral dealing with death better than non-Christians. God uses death to give us the opportunity to explain the gospel to nonbelievers. We lose our fear of death when we see it as an exclamation point instead of a period.

**To Illustrate**

Years ago, passengers on a boat in Lake Michigan were upset by the danger of a raging storm. By contrast, one of the passengers, evangelist D. L. Moody, seemed both quiet and calm. When asked how he could be so relaxed, he replied, "I have a sister in Chicago and one in heaven. I don't care which one I see first."

**To Meditate**

A bee sting can be a fearsome thing. But a bee loses its stinger when it stings and it can never cause pain again. Death, too, has been conquered—through Jesus Christ.

**To Pray**

Since you know where you're going when you die, ask God for an opportunity *this week* to show a friend who is fearful of death the victory there is in Jesus Christ.

# Lips that never lie are a testimony to our Father and our family.

**To Read**

> *Therefore, putting away lying, "Let each one of you speak truth with his neighbor," for we are members of one another.*
>
> —Ephesians 4:25

**To Consider**

Lying is often regarded as simply a lapse in judgment instead of a sin. The degree of wrongdoing seems to be measured by the size of the lie and whether or not anyone gets hurt by it. In one survey, 90 percent of those questioned said they lied regularly about matters they considered trivial.

Regarding untruths, Paul the apostle reduces the Christian's course of action to three simple words: "Putting away lying." Reflecting Zechariah 8:16, where the prophet sets forth the ethical obligations of a life of faith, Paul continues, "Let each one of you speak truth with his neighbor." Put simply, the word of a Christian ought to be his or her bond. Christians are called to be true in everything—including our behavior and speech. In our business dealings, we should present things as they are. In our personal convictions, we're to allow no space for pretense or sham.

Why the admonition? In the immediate context, Paul explains, "For we are members of one another." As brothers and sisters in the body of Christ, why would we deceive another member of our own family? We are to "put off . . . [our] former conduct" (Eph. 4:22) and "put on the new man" (v. 24). Truth, not lies, is to be the order of the day. Lying is unacceptable.

We daily cross paths with non-Christians who, as slaves of sin, have a propensity toward lying. In their sinful condition, they are related to Satan, the one who is a liar (John 8:44). As Christians, saved by grace, we must demonstrate to others that we march to the beat of a different drum. Lips that never lie are a testimony to our Father and our family.

**To Illustrate**

A twelve-year-old boy was called as a key witness in a lawsuit. One of the opposing lawyers said accusingly, "Your father told you what to say, didn't he?" The boy confessed that he had. The lawyer continued, "What were his instructions?" The boy replied, "Dad told me that the lawyers would try to tangle me up in my testimony, but if I would just be careful and tell the truth, I could say the same thing every time." As we speak the truth, Christians ought to say the same thing every time.

## To Meditate

If you want to give people an image of the One who is the Truth, then speak to them through truthful lips.

## To Pray

Ask God to make you into a person who so consistently speaks the truth that your words are always to be trusted.

## Day 22

*Believers who represent Christ well are noted for their tenderness, not their toughness.*

**To Read**

*Therefore be merciful, just as your Father also is merciful.*

—Luke 6:36

**To Consider**

"Big boys don't cry."

"Just wait! I'll have my chance to get even."

"I hope he falls on his face. It'll do him good."

"He deserves everything that has happened to him. I knew it would catch up with him."

"Nothing bothers me. I'm tough!"

How many times have you heard those or similar expressions? How tough people are, is sometimes determined by how big a bully they are.

Jesus Christ turns the tables on such ridiculous thinking. People who walk closely with Jesus Christ are keenly aware of His mercy. God the Father is so merciful that He extends kindness toward the thankful and the unthankful, makes the sun shine on the evil and the good, and sends rain on the just and the unjust. God's mercy keeps from us what we deserve and gives us instead what we don't deserve.

As recipients of God's mercy, believers ought to extend mercy to others. We should offer encouragement over condemnation, kindness instead of revenge, and an understanding spirit instead of a judgmental attitude. In contemporary society, a spirit of mercy is not often found in workplaces, homes, and neighborhoods. By extending mercy, believers give non-Christians an impression of what the Savior is like. Believers who represent Christ well are noted for their tenderness, not their toughness.

**To Illustrate**

A sensitive young man named William Herschel joined the British army, but deserted when the artillery shells began to fly. In time, he became a great astronomer and discovered a new planet. Summoned by King George, he knew that, despite his accomplishments, he was in great danger for having deserted the army in his younger years. Before the king would see him, Herschel was handed an envelope—which contained his royal pardon. When Herschel came before the king, the king explained, "Now we can talk, and you shall come up and live at Windsor Castle."

Herschel did not deny his guilt, nor did King George III withhold his mercy. As a recipient of mercy, William Herschel could now be merciful to others.

**To Meditate**

If your friend made a mess of life and needed help getting back on track, would your heart and home be an example of harshness or tenderness?

**To Pray**

At times when you are tempted to be unmerciful, ask God to help you reflect on specific ways He's been merciful to you—and then extend that same mercy in a practical way to others.

## Day 23

*Contentment is not found in having something we need, but through Someone we know.*

**To Read**

> *Not that I speak in regard to need, for I have learned in whatever state I am, to be content: I know how to be abased, and I know how to abound. Everywhere and in all things I have learned both to be full and to be hungry, both to abound and to suffer need. I can do all things through Christ who strengthens me.*

—Philippians 4:11–13

**To Consider**

A bigger house. A newer car. More land. A larger bank account. There's nothing wrong with having these things, but *everything* is wrong when we look to them for contentment. When that happens, the house is never big enough, and the car is never new enough. The search for contentment often ends badly in failed marriages, enormous debt, or even suicide.

Paul the apostle was delighted when the church at Philippi provided for his financial need. But he was quick to point out that their gift provided for his *need,* it did not provide for his *contentment.* Contentment was found in whom he had, not *what* he had.

Paul knew how to live humbly, and he knew how to enjoy prosperity. There were times when he could say, "I don't believe I can eat any more," and times when he was uncertain from where the next meal was coming. So why did his contentment never change even though his circumstances did?

He declares, "I can do all things through Christ who strengthens me." Hunger or prosperity—Paul could handle either through Christ. When we understand that truth, we understand why non-Christians are at such a loss. They have no inner strength to handle their outward circumstances.

Varied circumstances offer an opportunity for a Christian to demonstrate the contentment of a Christ-centered life. If more comes, we are grateful. If we have less, we are nonetheless satisfied. Provisions minister to our need, never to our contentment. Contentment is not found in having something we need, but through Someone we know.

**To Illustrate**

An elderly Christian was on his deathbed, so weak that he was often unconscious. During one of his lucid moments, he was asked about the cause of his perfect peace. He replied, "When I am able to think, I think of Jesus; and when I am unable to think of Him, I know He is thinking of me." The believer's contentment lies in thinking about and relying upon the One who is always thinking of us.

**To Meditate**

Some people live in an atmosphere of contentment, while others search for an atmosphere in which they can be content.

**To Pray**

Ask God for His strength to handle the moments when you have less than you need and the moments when you have more than you need. Then ask Him to use your day-to-day witness of contentment to introduce others to the Savior who is bigger than life's circumstances.

*Nobody is more impressive on the job than a citizen of the King displaying the manners of the court.*

## To Read

*Exhort bondservants to be obedient to their own masters, to be well pleasing in all things, not answering back, not pilfering, but showing all good fidelity, that they may adorn the doctrine of God our Savior in all things.*

—Titus 2:9

## To Consider

Next to your family, nobody spends more time around you than the people you work with. It's important that the Savior you claim to know is the Savior they see in you. A life taught at church on Sunday needs to be lived at work on Monday.

Slavery is no fun. Christian slaves in Paul's day

might have been tempted to think about how much their masters owed them. After all, the masters take away a slave's freedom, rob them of their strength, and withhold adequate compensation. But when Paul taught Titus how to instruct slaves, he spoke of what the slaves owed their masters.

He told slaves (employees in our day) that they were to be characterized by five things. They were to

- be obedient to their masters, characterized by submission, not rebellion.
- be well pleasing in all things—no exceptions and no excuses.
- not answer back—no place was to be given to grumbling.
- not steal—servants were to give, not take.
- show all good fidelity—"Trust me" was to be a character trait, not a cliché.

But why? Because it makes the Savior look beautiful. Paul concludes, "That they may adorn the doctrine of God our Savior in all things." As jewels enhance the beauty of a crown, a conscientious employee adorns the doctrine of God.

Christian servants radiate the glory of the gospel, a gospel so powerful it could take slaves—degraded beings in the eyes of the world—and transform them into obedient, honest, serious-minded men and women. Nobody is more impressive on the job than a citizen of the King displaying the manners of the court.

## To Illustrate

Thomas Jefferson once said that in hiring men he considered three questions: Is he honest? Will he work? Is he loyal? If your employer and coworkers were to answer those questions about you, what would they say?

## To Meditate

If your coworkers don't see your Christianity at work, you give them reason to wonder whether Christianity works.

## To Pray

Ask God to make you such an example of Christlikeness at work that others will notice the difference between you and your non-Christian coworkers—a difference that could open doors for the gospel.

*Day 25*

*There is something special about Christians who view themselves as number two and others as number one.*

## To Read

*Let nothing be done through selfish ambition or conceit, but in lowliness of mind let each esteem others better than himself.*

—Philippians 2:3

## To Consider

What strikes you about many people is not their humility; it's their conceit. Will Rogers once said, "I always like to hear a man talk about himself, because then I never hear anything but good."

In Philippians 2, Paul addresses the unity that should exist among believers. But he makes it clear that the basis for unity is not a method—it's a mind-set. He exhorts, "Let nothing be done through selfish ambition or conceit." Selfish ambition and conceit typify people who desire to promote themselves. People with selfish ambition and conceit lose friends instead of making friends.

After describing the condition, Paul gives the cure: "But in lowliness of mind let each esteem others better than himself." The cure in a word is *humility*. Humble people consider others more important than themselves. In the minds of humble people, others are number one and they are number two.

How does that spirit of humility impact non-Christians? Some non-Christians believe that Christians are conceited. They sometimes say, "Christians act like they are related to God Himself." Of course we do, because we are! Non-Christians sometimes say, "Christians have the audacity to think they are going to heaven." Of course we do, because we are! But if humility accompanies our justifiable confidence—if we focus on others instead of ourselves—we'll stand in marked contrast to most others around us. There is something special about Christians who view themselves as number two and others as number one.

## To Illustrate

In 1994, Thurman Thomas sat on the Buffalo Bills' bench with his head bowed and his hands covering his face. His team had just suffered its fourth straight Super Bowl loss, and Thomas's three fumbles had helped seal their awful fate. Suddenly, standing before him was Emmitt Smith, the Dallas Cowboys' star running back, who had just been voted the Most Valuable Player for Super Bowl XXVIII. Smith, with his small goddaughter in his arms, looked at her and said, "I want you to meet the greatest running back in the NFL, Mr. Thurman Thomas." Paul would likewise tell believers, "In lowliness of mind, let each esteem others better than himself."

## To Meditate

People who live contagiously do not concentrate on building monuments to themselves; they focus on building up others.

## To Pray

Ask God to cause the importance of others to increase in your mind and the importance of yourself to decrease. Ask Him to give you an opportunity *today* to tell somebody how important he or she is to you.

*Day 26*

# We no longer need to do the things we used to do, because we are no longer the people we used to be.

## To Read

*For this is the will of God, your sanctification: that you should abstain from sexual immorality; that each of you should know how to possess his own vessel in sanctification and honor, not in passion of lust, like the Gentiles who do not know God.*

—1 Thessalonians 4:3–5

## To Consider

When basketball star Magic Johnson confessed to having the HIV virus, he told *Sports Illustrated,* "The problem is that I can't pinpoint the time, the place or the woman. It's a matter of numbers. . . . I confess that often I arrived in LA, in 1979, and did my best to accommodate as many women as I could—most of them through unprotected sex."

As Paul wrote to the believers of Thessalonica, he

knew that they inhabited a Greek city where sexual sin was the order of the day. Men sought sexual satisfaction outside of the marriage bond, and the pagan religions fostered sexual immorality. Female priests in the temple performed sexual rituals with the men.

Paul acknowledges that nonbelievers engage in immoral behavior for a simple reason—they do not know God. Consequently, they conduct themselves in what he terms the "passion of lust." God has called Christians to a higher standard. Sexual immorality is out of the question for people who have been sanctified or "set apart" by the Holy Spirit. In its place, a life of holiness is our day-to-day goal.

Paul wrote that a husband is instructed to "possess his own vessel in sanctification and honor." The word *vessel* was used by rabbis to refer to one's wife. Thus, a person's sexual desires are to be satisfied by one person—and within the bond of marriage.

Non-Christians should see that believers live by a moral standard—not based on regulations but on a relationship. As they witness our fidelity rather than infidelity, we may have opportunities to explain that we no longer need to do the things we used to do, because we are no longer the people we used to be.

**To Illustrate**

On the night that Jamaican slaves were set free in 1838, a large mahogany coffin was made, and a grave was dug. Into the coffin, the liberated slaves threw reminders of their former lives of slavery: whips, handcuffs, torture irons, and fragments of a tread-mill. Then the lid of the coffin was fastened down. At the stroke of midnight, the coffin was lowered into the ground and buried. Then the liberated slaves sang, "Praise God from whom all blessings flow." Thanks to their new freedom, they were keenly aware that they need not do the things they used to do, because they were no longer the people they used to be.

## To Meditate

The decision to be pure does not depend on your mate, but on your mind.

## To Pray

Ask God to give you a biblical mind-set toward sexual purity. Ask Him to help you say no to temptation, so that your life will be a contrast to those who view sex as a god instead of as a gift from God.

*Believers who say good things about others have a platform to say great things about their Savior.*

## To Read

> *To speak evil of no one, to be peaceable, gentle, showing all humility to all men.*
>
> —Titus 3:2

## To Consider

Ever notice how easy it is to slander? Just catch someone making a small mistake, then blow it out of proportion and put it on the gossip hot line. Others will help spread the rumor. No education is required, and no training is necessary. The only prerequisite for slander is that we give license to our depraved, sinful nature. No wonder we're so good at it.

But where the world gives a green light, God puts up a stop sign. Insults and abusive language are out of place for anyone, but especially for believers who are indwelled by the Holy Spirit. When Paul lists seven qualities that should characterize Christians, he includes "to speak evil of no one."

Does that mean Christians cannot "call 'em like they see 'em"? Not at all. In fact, plain speaking is a mark of integrity and a demonstration of character. What Paul is addressing is the issue of insults, humiliating and destructive comments, and abusive language. Christians are to be "peaceable, gentle, showing all humility to all men."

Why? As Paul goes on to explain, we ourselves were once in an ugly, sinful condition, and yet we received the grace of God. God could have pointed out all of our wrongs and then punished us. Instead, on the basis of Christ's substitutionary death and subsequent resurrection, He forgives those who trust Him as their Savior. It is easier to talk to nonbelievers about God's grace when we have demonstrated that same grace toward others. Believers who say good things about others have a platform to say great things about their Savior.

**To Illustrate**

Some women in the church held a sewing session for a needy family. When one lady was asked if she could assist, she replied, "I'm not a very good seamstress. About all I can do is rip and tear up." Christians who speak well of others are in contrast to those who "rip and tear up."

**To Meditate**

All it takes to make a mountain out of a molehill is a little more dirt.

**To Pray**

Ask God to convict you by His Spirit when you are tempted to imitate the slanderous language of the world. As you "speak evil of no one," ask God to open doors for the gospel.

*Believers face discouragement knowing there is hope, while nonbelievers face discouragement and wonder what hope there is.*

## To Read

*Why are you cast down, O my soul? And why are you disquieted within me? Hope in God, for I shall yet praise Him for the help of His countenance.*

—Psalm 42:5

## To Consider

Discouragement shows no partiality. It hits people of all ages, races, occupations, and income brackets. The only difference is how we handle it.

In Psalm 42 and 43, the psalmist engages in a life and death struggle with discouragement. Exiled to the northern part of Palestine, he yearns to return to the temple in Jerusalem, but for now he cannot go.

Ten times he asks the question that is in every aching heart: "Why God, why?" Three times he asks the question, "Why are you in despair (cast down)? Why are you disturbed (disquieted)?"

Then the psalmist answers—there is hope in God. His hope lies in a real presence, not just a feeling. His hope is in a Being who eternally demonstrates His lovingkindness (42:8) and delivers His children from unjust men (43:1). As long as He is there, that is all that matters.

What hope do non-Christians have when they have never met the One they need most? Why *wouldn't* a non-Christian say, "What hope is there?" When believers respond to discouragement by recognizing that God *is* there, it can provide a powerful and persuasive testimony to nonbelievers. We can introduce our lost friends to the One who is the only hope of heaven, and we can explain that God is also our only hope on earth.

What a contrast! Believers face discouragement knowing there is hope, while nonbelievers face discouragement and wonder what hope there is.

**To Illustrate**

As German bombs rained down on England during World War II, the situation grew desperate. Hearts were filled with discouragement and thoughts of defeat. Then Winston Churchill's voice came over the radio. It caused the nation to take heart and restored morale to a people ready to quit. On a spiritual level, believers have hope in a God whose voice still rings out through the pages of His Word. In moments of discouragement, Christians are a testimony to those who have never met God or heard His voice.

## To Meditate

When you are discouraged, remember that your hope is in the One who enters those moments with you and whose strength will lead you through them.

## To Pray

Pray for a non-Christian who is going through a time of discouragement. Ask God to give you an opportunity *this week* to speak to him or her, using your own testimony of God's faithfulness during times of discouragement as a bridge to the gospel.

## Day 29

*We help others most when we share truth, but with grace.*

**To Read**

*And the Word became flesh and dwelt among us, and we beheld His glory, the glory as of the only begotten of the Father, full of grace and truth.*

—John 1:14

**To Consider**

Some Christians go to extremes in their interactions with nonbelievers. Some have grace but without the balance of truth. They would never say to anyone, "You're a sinner." Other believers speak the truth but without the balance of grace. It's not *what* they say that hurts, but the way they say it. They speak to non-Christians in a way that's uncaring at best and callous at worst.

In describing the person of Christ, John makes it clear that Jesus was God in human flesh. Then he adds "full of grace and truth." These two qualities of

Christ's character are repeated again and again in the pages of John's gospel.

Jesus Christ was truthful when He talked with the Samaritan woman: "You have well said, 'I have no husband,' for you have had five husbands, and the one whom you now have is not your husband" (John 4:17–18). He confronted the Pharisees, saying, "You are of your father the devil" (8:44). Yet He was full of grace. He said to the woman caught in adultery, "Neither do I condemn you; go and sin no more" (8:11). Truth and grace must always accompany one another.

Some non-Christians don't appreciate the truth in any form. But even those who are willing to listen want to hear truth expressed with kindness. It's one thing to speak honestly and directly to nonbelievers, but we should speak the truth with love and grace. Every Christian should desire to hear from their non-Christian friends, "Thanks for being honest with me. What I really appreciated, though, was the way you said it." We help others most when we share truth, but with grace.

**To Illustrate**

Duc de Richelieu, the French statesman, was a man noted for his truthful but courteous manner. It is reported that an individual once applied for a job, knowing he'd be turned down. Richelieu's manner was such that the applicant felt it was worth being turned down just to hear how graciously Richelieu expressed himself. That combination of truth and grace can make an eternal difference in the lives of non-Christians.

**To Meditate**

When properly mixed, grace and truth are two ingredients that help us serve a well-balanced message to non-Christians.

**To Pray**

Ask God to use His Word, along with your spiritual growth and experience, to show you how to approach people with the truth of the gospel, but in a manner that demonstrates how much you care.

*Getting into the Bible
will do you no good,
unless the Bible gets into
you.*

## To Read

> *But be doers of the word, and not hearers only, de-
> ceiving yourselves. For if anyone is a hearer of the
> word and not a doer, he is like a man observing his
> natural face in a mirror; for he observes himself,
> goes away, and immediately forgets what kind of
> man he was. But he who looks into the perfect law
> of liberty and continues in it, and is not a forgetful
> hearer but a doer of the work, this one will be blessed
> in what he does.*

—James 1:22–25

## To Consider

Becoming a Christian means trusting Christ as
the only way to heaven. Growing as a Christian
means learning more about Him. An excellent way
to learn about Christ is by reading the Bible. But

let's not overlook the obvious. We'll never grow if what we read in the Bible stays in the Bible.

James is writing to Christians who were undergoing severe trials. Because James was concerned that these believers might only *hear* the Word, he admonishes them also to *heed* the Word.

If we hear the Word but don't heed it, we are like the man who sees his face in a mirror, studies it for a moment, then goes his way. The phrase "he forgets what kind of man he was" implies that the man doesn't really care. The mirror has had no impact upon him.

In contrast are people who are doers and not merely hearers. As they grow, they develop spiritual maturity—the ability to look at life through God's eyes instead of their own. Their happiness is observable to all, including non-Christians.

As active believers read the Bible, God through His Word removes from their lives what should not be there and puts in what should be. But getting into the Bible will do you no good, unless the Bible gets into you.

### To Illustrate

D. L. Moody once said, "The Bible was not given to increase our knowledge but to change our lives."

### To Meditate

People who live contagiously read the Scriptures

and then translate its truth into daily life—a language that non-Christians find very easy to read.

**To Pray**

Ask God to give you a consistent time in the Bible. Each week as you live the Word, ask God for opportunities to introduce others to the Author of the Bible.

*Something is different
about people who are
holding things instead of
letting things hold them.*

## To Read

> *Command those who are rich in this present age
> not to be haughty, nor to trust in uncertain riches
> but in the living God, who gives us richly all things
> to enjoy.*

> —*1 Timothy 6:17*

## To Consider

Nowhere does the Bible condemn wealth. It simply encourages the right use of it.

Paul, in writing to Timothy, warns religious teachers about the danger of viewing the ministry as a way to wealth. He then turns to address those in the church who had large estates and considerable means. His warning is twofold. First, they were not to be "haughty," high-minded, or proud. They were not to consider themselves more important than others or pat themselves on the back simply because of their healthy bank balances. Moreover, they were not to put their trust in worldly riches, which could be here today and gone tomorrow. As someone once said, "Money talks. The problem is, it always says good-bye." No, their trust was to be in "the living God, who gives us richly all things to enjoy." All their possessions were gifts from Him to manage and enjoy. These gifts were to be their servants, not their masters. The people were to use things, not allow things to use them.

In our society, where many non-Christians hold the view "He who dies with the most toys wins," such an approach to materialism catches people's attention. Those without Christ are awestruck by believers who enjoy what they own but are not possessed by it. Believers can take advantage of this attention to talk about whom they trust, not what they trust. Something is different about people who are holding things instead of letting things hold them.

**To Illustrate**

A man and his wife live in a stunning home in Seattle. Their house is built mainly of glass and is decorated with glass artifacts of all kinds—including sinks, shelves, and mantelpieces. It would be understandable if this couple lived in fear of something breaking and carefully guarded their property. The opposite is the case. They enjoy inviting visitors to roam freely throughout their home. The husband also collects Native American crafts and has donated his entire collection to the Seattle Art Museum. Intent on sharing, not hoarding, he explained, "I'm not an owner. I'm a caretaker."

## To Meditate

When you view everything you have, do you see yourself as a manager or an owner?

## To Pray

Ask God to help you hold everything you have in a loose grip, recognizing that all things are temporary gifts to enjoy. Ask Him to use you as a witness to those who may have everything but Him.

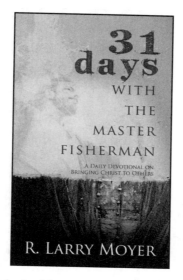

## 31 Days with the Master Fisherman
*A Daily Devotional on Bringing Christ to Others*
by R. Larry Moyer

Since many things are better caught than taught, this book encourages readers to spend time in reflection and meditation on the subjects of discipleship and evangelism. As we spend time considering the things closest to Jesus' heart, we will catch His vision for sharing the Good News.

This one-month daily devotional book is designed to encourage all believers to join in the Great Commission to share the Good News and to improve each person's skills in the greatest fishing expedition of all times!

978-0-8254-3569-0 / 96 pp.

## Welcome to the Family!

*Understanding Your New Relationship to God and Others*
by EvanTell Resources; Foreword by R. Larry Moyer

Some of the most commonly asked questions by new
believers are answered: How do I know I'm going
to heaven? How does God talk to me? What does it
mean to follow Christ? and How will my relationships
change? A practical and easy-to-follow guide to growing in the Christian faith.

978-0-8254-3176-0 / 80 pp.